CONTACTS:

In case of an *accident*, *emergency* or just *advice* these some useful numbers to ring for information and help.

NHS Direct 0845 4647

Your call will automatically be put through to your nearest centre and will be charged at local rates (*May be more from a mobile*).

www.nhsdirect.nhs.uk

Your local Health Visitor can be contacted via your GP practice.

Add your GP's number here

Your local Fire Service can be contacted for advice on fire prevention.

Child Accident Prevention Trust (CAPT) 020 7608 3828
A charity committed to reducing childhood injury.
www.capt.org.uk

First Aid Courses
British Red Cross 0845 608 6888
St. John Ambulance 0870 010 4950

Useful numbers in your area:

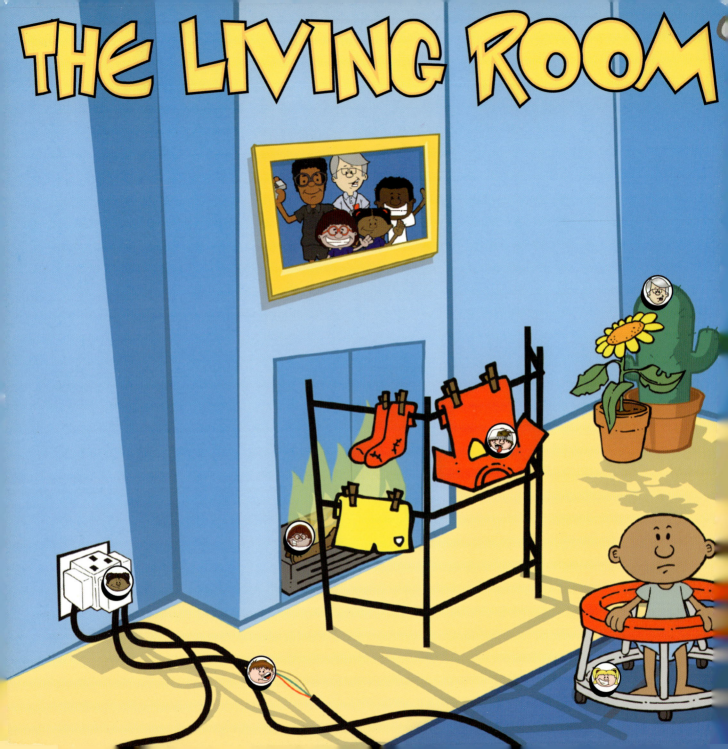

THE LIVING ROOM

Check all house plants, some may be toxic to your child.

Never hang clothes to dry over fires or heaters, they might fall and catch fire.

Do not overload electrical sockets.

Always use a fireguard for all heaters and fires.

Replace old or worn flexes, they could start a fire.

Do not use baby walkers - research shows that they do not teach children to walk, but they can tip over very easily throwing the baby out.

Keep hot drinks out of the way of children, hot water can scald 20 minutes after it has boiled.

Keep cigarettes and ashtrays out of reach of children. If you have to smoke, try not to do it in the same room as children - smoking will damage their health.

Keep matches out of reach of children.

Keep candles out of reach of children and extinguish them completely on leaving a room.

Alcohol is toxic to young children, keep it out of reach or in a locked cupboard.

THE KITCHEN

Use door stops to avoid small fingers getting trapped. Remember to remove them and close all doors at night as a fire safety precaution.

Avoid using chip pans - a common cause of home fires. Use oven chips or a deep fat frier instead.

Use all back rings when cooking and turn all pan handles away from the edge.

Never leave a hot iron unattended. Unplug it immediately after use and put it on a high surface while it cools down. Remember to put the flex and plug out of reach as well. Consider ironing when the kids are in bed.

Don't use the microwave for heating milk or baby food, it can produce dangerous hotspots.

Always strap little ones into high chairs and stay with them whilst they are eating.

This meat needs to be stored in the fridge. Food should be stored correctly to avoid food poisoning.

Don't leave sharp knives near the edge of the worktop.

Use kettles with short or curly flexes and keep the flexes well out of sight and reach of toddlers.

Keep plastic bags out of the way to prevent a child from suffocating.

HALL AND STAIRS

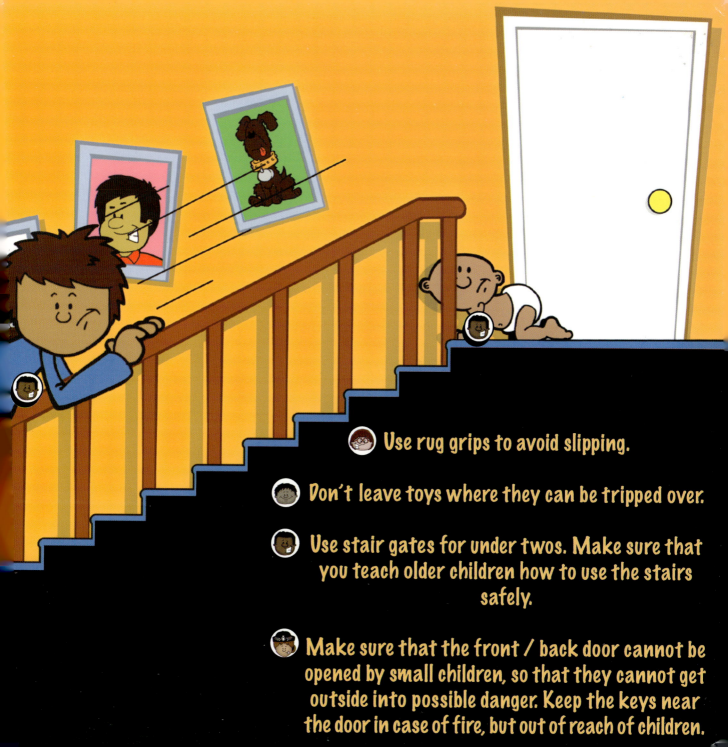

- A baby should never be left to feed alone from a propped up bottle as they may choke and not be able to push the bottle away.

- Throw away damaged or broken toys.

- Put safety catches onto windows to stop children from falling out.

- Never use duvets or pillows for children under one as they could suffocate.

- Keep small toys out of reach of babies and very young children as they could choke on them.

- Don't leave anything on the floor that could cause someone to slip or trip.

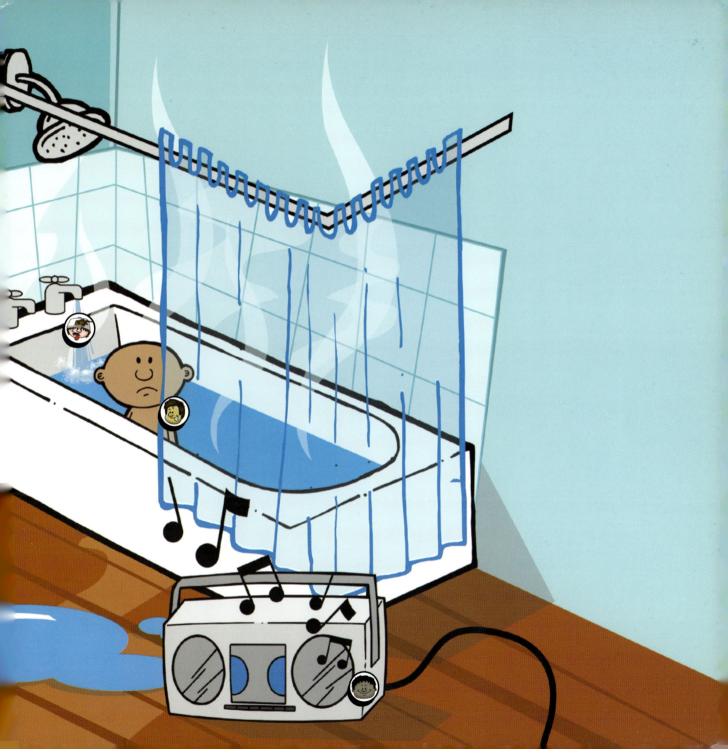

THE BATHROOM

- Never leave a baby or young child alone in the bath, they can drown in just a few centimetres of water very quickly with no noise or struggle.

- Water from the hot tap can scald. Always run the cold water before the hot and don't leave the hot tap running.

- Electrical appliances should not be used in the bathroom. You could get an electrical shock.

- Keep all cleaning materials out of reach of children.

- Lock medicines in a cabinet or cupboard out of reach of children as they could mistake them for sweets.
  Don't let young children see you taking tablets – they may try to copy you.

- Always put down a mat or towel when bathing or showering to stop the floor becoming a slippery hazard.